Please send any correspondence regarding permissions to:
UniversityOfHealthCare
PO Box 48891A
Los Angeles, CA 90048

ISBN: 1932634886

Library of Congress Catalog Number: 2003113516

UniversityOfHealthCare website: www.uohc.com

GW00514820

Contents

Introduction   1

The Authors   2

OSHA Workplace Violence   4

OSHA Regulations   26

Introduction

This product consists of a combination of this manual and a CD. The manual is a summary of the important points presented more interactively on the CD.

When you place the CD in your computer, it should load automatically and install with some simple steps. If it does not start automatically, open up Windows Explorer (from Start, Programs, Accessories) and navigate to the setup file with the abstract arrow icon on your CD drive. Then double click it. It will then install on your computer. After that, you may open the program by clicking on Start, Programs, and then the name of the program. This will open the program file. After you run it the first time, an icon will automatically be added to your desktop.

This program is protected with anti-piracy software. The product is licensed to one user on one computer. As a result, you will need to take a few minutes to license your product with a password key. You will have some time to use the program before it stops working.

You must have Internet Explorer 4.0 or higher running on your computer. Supported operating systems are Windows 95, 98, 98 SE, ME, 2000, or XP. You will need Internet access to e-mail us your key and receive a password key. License is for one user on one computer. An additional computer owned by the same user will generally be approved at the discretion of the publisher.

You have a unique serial number to identify your product. Please keep this number carefully. We can do nothing for you if you lose it before you have registered it and unlocked the software.

For any questions about your license or the program, contact us at license@uohc.com.

About the Authors

M. Daniel Farb, CEO of UniversityOfHealthCare and
UniversityOfBusiness, is a leader in the field of interactive
management and healthcare e-learning. He received a BA in
English Literature from Yale (where he set an academic record
and studied with writers like Robert Penn Warren), an M.D.
from Boston University, a degree in Executive Management
from the Anderson School of Business at UCLA, and is
currently working on a degree at UCLA in International Trade.
He is a practicing ophthalmologist. He also has received two
patents in ophthalmology and is working on others, has worked
with the World Health Organization in Geneva and the National
Institutes of Health in Washington, D.C. He has written
scientific and popular articles, and has worked as a newspaper
reporter. He helped Dr. Robbins edit one of the editions of
Robbins' "Pathology" textbook for readability. He wrote an
article on humor for the Massachusetts Review. He has
experience in theater and television, including acting, directing,
and stage-managing. He has programmed his own patient
records database. He has written and edited hundreds of e-
learning courses.

Dr. Farb is a member of the American Academy of
Ophthalmology, the Union of American Physicians and
Dentists, the AOJS, the American Association of Physicians
and Surgeons, the ASTD (American Society for Training and
Development), the E-Learning Forum, the Southern California
Biomedical Council, the PDA (Parenteral Drug Association),
and the Medical Marketing Association.

BRUCE GORDON is the Creative Director for
UniversityOfHealthCare, LLC, and plays an important role in
writing the more creative projects, especially those with stories.

After receiving a BA in Economics from UCLA, he began a freelance writing career that included technical writing (such as a manual for Princess Cruise Lines), stand-up comedy routines for nationally known comedians, and screenplay writing. He has done production support work with famous Hollywood personalities on such well-known productions as Aaron Spelling's "Dynasty" and "Love Boat" TV shows.

An audio-visual software specialist, he is a versatile artist, with published works in a variety of media, including music, motion graphics, and digital video short film.

OSHA Workplace Violence

Workplace violence is common and rising. Fifty-seven percent of companies responding to a survey said violence occurred in their workplace during the last 3 three years.
A recent survey said 36 percent of violent work incidents are triggered by family or marital problems, 24 percent by stress, 18 percent by getting fired.
Most of this results in nothing more than pushing or verbal threats.

Roughly 30 percent of workplace homicides are cases of clients attacking employees, according to the National Institute for Occupational Safety and Health (NIOSH). Stranger versus employee violence (armed robbery, for example), makes up 60 percent of workplace homicides. Cases where an employee attacks another employee make up about 10 percent of workplace homicides.

* Nov. 2, 1999: Xerox copy repairman Byran Uyesugi, 40, allegedly kills seven co-workers in Honolulu. He surrenders after a five-hour standoff.

* Aug. 5, 1999: Truck driver Alan Miller, 34, allegedly kills three current and former co-workers in Pelham, Ala. He is awaiting trial.

* July 29, 1999: Investor Mark O. Barton, 44, kills nine people and wounds 13 others at two brokerage firms in Atlanta, then kills himself.

Many big companies have begun to teach their employees about the potential for violence in the workplace. They cite the potential risks, as well as the importance of reporting signs of violent behavior as early as possible. Some corporations take a zero-tolerance approach, firing any employee who threatens, intimidates, harasses, stalks, or in any way inflicts physical violence at the worksite.

The aim of these policies is to rid a firm's building(s) of people who could be dangerous. They also strive, despite any resultant inconvenience, to fortify the building(s) with the following:
* Fewer exits
* Fewer entry points
* Much tighter security

Other firms have obtained court orders to prevent former employees from coming within a certain range of an office.

Yet, not all employers have developed policies to deal with the potentials for violence on the job. Smaller businesses are especially vulnerable, as two-thirds of American businesses work without a formal violence prevention plan. All businesses need to analyze this issue, and make a determination to put procedures in place.

No policy can guarantee freedom from violent incidents. However, they can assist in helping to uncover problem people before they can hurt regular, law-abiding personnel.

For this reason, it behooves a company to train its work force with contingency plans.

A number of government agencies provide information and recommendations aimed at dealing with the workplace violence issue.

Some of these include the following:

* U.S. Office of Personnel Management
* National Institute for Occupational Safety and Health (NIOSH)
* Federal Protective Service
* Occupational Safety and Health Administration (OSHA)

OSHA (associated with the U.S. Department of Labor) has established procedures to help employers develop workplace violence prevention programs. They aren't regulations or even standards, but they're excellent as recommendations to battle the problem.

OSHA does, however, have the authority to cite and fine a firm if its employees are denied a safe working environment.

OSHA's statistics indicate that healthcare facilities are especially prone to workplace violence. To protect these workers, the administration published specific guidelines in 1996 for this industry.

This document is entitled, "Occupational Safety and Health Administration: Guidelines for Preventing Workplace Violence for Health Care and Social Service Workers, OSHA 3148, 1996".

Of course, any industry's facilities can and must use many of the same principles to protect their workers.

These guidelines are available at OSHA's website: www.osha.gov and at www.healthsafetyinfo.com/resources/0125a001.cfm. (Reprinted at the end of this manual.)

OSHA suggests that a firm should create a written prevention plan.

Larger organizations can integrate a written workplace violence program into its comprehensive health and safety SOPs (standard operating procedures). When the facility is smaller, an acceptable program doesn't necessarily need to take the form of substantial written documentation. Just make sure, in any case, that the policy goals and objectives are clear. Also, be sure that they match the size and intricacies of the intended workplace operation.

Every employee has to be given a chance to review the prevention program, as well as to be informed of its commencement date.

PREVENTION

It's not really a good idea to count solely upon the use of "personality profiles" to predict whether or not an individual has the potential toward violent behavior. When these blanket categorizations are made, violence isn't foretold or forecast. But what does tend to occur is the stereotyping of employees, which is unfair and destructive.

However, a conscientious and compassionate awareness of personalities with the potential toward violence can assist firms in trying to provide a safe working environment for their employees. Some examples:
* Loners
* Men in their forties
* People with compulsive habits or hobbies

"Early warning signs" are also used to predict the possibility of workplace violence. Just as with personality profiles, these conditions must be judged in a comprehensive manner that includes sensitivity toward personnel, even those exhibiting the questionable behavior.
* Battling stress at home and on the job
* Being in therapy
* Death in the family
* Suffering form mental illness
* Facing a layoff or other loss of employment

Why shouldn't you automatically assume that an employee facing these conditions will become violent?
* Every person experiences illness, stress or loss at some point in life.
* All but an extreme few people get through their difficult times without resorting to violence.

Treating a troubled employee with fear and paranoia about violence isn't the recommended policy. It's better if managers receive training on how to be supportive of their employees during their hard times, especially when it comes to bereavement or mental illness.
In spite of the preceding caveat, there are some definite "early warning signs" that shouldn't be ignored; in fact, they should be reported and dealt with immediately. Some of these include employees who:
* Threaten revenge
* Have difficulty with authority
* Become angry or upset easily
* Act paranoid and do things like fill notebooks with what they consider insults
* Don't see humor in any situation
* Don't show sensitivity in any form

* Openly speak about weapons in the context of "teaching people a lesson"
* Often speak of violent movies or books that they continually see or read
* Threaten to sue often

It's important to be aware of disputes between coworkers, and with customers/clients. These have sometimes escalated into violence after civil attempts at resolution have failed.

What are some other precipitating events that have led some individuals to workplace violence?
* Being passed over for promotion
* Rejection of a relationship
* Discrimination
* Firing
Some studies indicate that a worker who's prone to violence could use the anniversary of his or her termination date to return for revenge.

What are some of the other definite signs that should raise suspicion of the possibility that an employee may become violent?
* Direct or veiled threats of harm
* Intimidating, belligerent, harassing, bullying, or other inappropriate and aggressive behavior
* Numerous conflicts with supervisors and other employees
* Bringing a weapon to the workplace, brandishing a weapon in the workplace, making inappropriate references to guns, or fascination with weapons
* Statements showing fascination with incidents of workplace violence, statements indicating approval of the use of violence to resolve a problem, or statements indicating identification with perpetrators of workplace homicides

* Statements indicating desperation (over family, financial, and other personal problems) to the point of contemplating suicide
* Drug/alcohol abuse
* Extreme changes in behaviors

Managers and fellow employees should never ignore these signs, since each one clearly shows that something is wrong. Investigated within the proper context (with the aforementioned compassion and sensitivity), these indicators may help identify and deal with problems before violence occurs.

It's best if management and other employees can work with a staff member (or an incident response team) established to specialize with workplace violence issues.

What are four main components of a good workplace violence protection program?
* Management commitment and employee involvement
* Worksite analysis
* Hazard prevention and control
* Safety and health training

The following are some areas in which facility managers need to show commitment:
* A system of accountability for involved managers, supervisors, and employees.
* A comprehensive program of medical and psychological counseling and debriefing for employees experiencing or witnessing assaults and other violent incidents.
* Demonstrated organizational concern for employee emotional and physical safety and health.
* Equal commitment to worker safety and health and patient/client safety.

* Assigned responsibility for the various aspects of the workplace violence prevention program to ensure that all managers, supervisors, and employees understand their obligations.
* Commitment to support and implement appropriate recommendations from safety and health committees.
* Appropriate allocation of authority and resources to all responsible parties.

A facility's employees also must be involved and committed. Their contributions and feedback can help in the design, implementation, and evaluation of a successful health and safety program.

Specific employee involvement should include the following areas:
* Understanding and complying with the workplace violence prevention program and other safety and security measures.
* Participation in an employee complaint or suggestion procedure covering safety and security concerns.
* Prompt and accurate reporting of violent incidents.
* Participation on safety and health committees or teams that receive reports of violent incidents or security problems, make facility inspections, and respond with recommendations for corrective strategies.
* Create and disseminate a clear policy of zero tolerance for workplace violence, verbal and nonverbal threats, and related actions. Managers, supervisors, co-workers, clients, patients, and visitors must be advised of this policy.
* Ensure that no reprisals are taken against an employee who reports or experiences workplace violence.

* Affirm management commitment to a worker-supportive environment that places as much importance on employee safety and health as on serving the patient or client.
* Set up a company briefing as part of the initial effort to address such issues as preserving safety, supporting affected employees, and facilitating recovery.
Specific areas in which management and supervisors should receive training:
* How to reduce security hazards and to be certain that proper training is given to employees
* How to recognize a potentially hazardous situation
* How to make any necessary changes in the physical plant, patient care treatment program, and staffing policy and procedures to reduce or eliminate the hazards.

Security staff and personnel should be given special training regarding the types of customers or clients that the facility will interface with. For hospital and clinic facilities, security workers need to be taught about:
* The psychological components of handling aggressive and abusive clients
* Types of disorders
* Ways to handle aggression and defuse hostile situations

An evaluation also needs to be included in the training program. The items that should be reviewed and evaluated annually by the responsible coordinator or team are the:
* Content of training
* Methods of training
* Frequency of training

Program evaluation can include:
* Interviews with supervisors and/or employees
* Testing and observing

* Reviewing reports of behavior of individuals in threatening situations

All employees need to comprehend a concept called "Universal Precautions for Violence."
* Violence should be expected but it also can be avoided or mitigated through preparation.
 * Personnel need to learn how to keep physical interventions in workplace altercations to the minimum level possible, unless enough numbers of staff or emergency response team members and security personnel exist.
* The probability of preventing assault can also be enhanced by frequent training.

Depending on the severity of the risks, training topics can involve:
* Management of Assaultive Behavior
* Professional Assault Response Training
* Police assault avoidance programs
* Personal safety training (e.g., avoidance awareness, and ways to prevent assaults

What other training topics should the program cover?
* The workplace violence prevention policy
* Risk factors that cause or contribute to assaults
* Early recognition of escalating behavior or recognition of warning signs or situations that may lead to assaults
* Ways of preventing or diffusing volatile situations or aggressive behavior, managing anger, and appropriately using medications as chemical restraints
* Information on multicultural diversity to develop sensitivity to racial and ethnic issues and differences

* A standard response action plan for violent situations, including availability of assistance, response to alarm systems, and communication procedures
* How to deal with hostile persons other than patients and clients, such as relatives and visitors
* Progressive behavior control methods and safe methods of restraint application or escape
* The location and operation of safety devices such as alarm systems, along with the required maintenance schedules and procedures.
* Ways to protect oneself and coworkers, including use of the "buddy system."
* Policies and procedures for reporting an recordkeeping
* Policies and procedures for obtaining medical care, counseling, workers' compensation or legal assistance after a violent episode or injury

De-escalation suggestions:
--Don't use body language that implies that you are confronting the individual:
--Don't face him directly, don't stare into his face, don't invade his personal space, and don't try to touch.

Speak in a way that discourages aggression:
--Use listening techniques. Repeating back part of what a person says for clarification shows the aggressive person you are trying to understand his message.
--Never show disrespect for his feelings. ("You're wrong to interpret your firing as a sign the boss didn't like you." Instead: "I'm sure that being fired must have been a great disappointment to you.")
--Don't threaten with consequences.
--Speak slowly and quietly.

WORKSITE ANALYSIS

Every facility should perform a worksite analysis. An
assessment team should be established to...
*Study the facility's potential for workplace violence
* Determine the best preventative measures

What should the analysis include?
* Studying employee tasks
* Identifying hazards, conditions, operations, and situations that
could lead to violence.
* Evaluating existing security systems
* Reviewing injury and illness records and workers'
compensation claims to identify patterns of assaults
* Developing screening surveys to encourage comments from
employees on what security improvements need to be made.

In analyzing the worksite, program coordinators should
exercise common sense and take steps to locate hazards, or
potential hazards. Facility operations, procedures, and
locations that could lend themselves to workplace violence
hazards need to be looked at in particular.

It can be a good idea to put together a task force to do this
assessment and to try and figure out the proper courses of
preventative measures.

This threat assessment team needs to be composed of
representatives from the following areas of the facility:
* Senior management
* Operations
* Employee assistance
* Security
* Occupational safety and health

* Legal
* Human resources staff

Specific records should be reviewed to identify instances of workplace violence as during records analysis and tracking. What are they?
* Medical records
* Safety records
* Workers' compensation records
* Insurance records, including OSHA 200 log

Employee and police reports of incidents or near-incidents of assaultive behavior should also be reviewed. This could illuminate assault trends related to specific:
* Unit activities
* Workstations
* Time of day
* Departments
* Units
* Job titles

This information can help uncover how often these incidents happen and how severe they have been. Measuring improvement is easier when these trends are used to establish a baseline.

It's also helpful to get data from other businesses in the same industry, as well as trade associations, community, and civic groups. The best methods involve tracing injury, incident, and potential violence trends over the course of several years.

Periodic inspections of the workplace and evaluations of employee tasks should be used to identify certain items that could lead to violence:

* Hazards
* Conditions
* Operations
* Situations

What other areas should the team or coordinator analyze?
* Violent incidents
-The characteristics of assailants and victims
-An account of what happened before and during the incident
-The relevant details of the situation and its outcome
-Police reports and recommendations
-Jobs or locations with the greatest risk of violence
-Processes and procedures that put employees at risk of assault,
including how often and when
* High-risk factors
-Types of clients or patients (including those with psychiatric
conditions or those disoriented by drugs, alcohol, or stress)
-Physical risk factors of the building
-Isolated locations or job activities
-Lighting problems
-Lack of phones and other communication devices, areas of
easy, unsecured access
-Areas with previous security problems
* The rate of success with existing security measures. Take
action that corresponds with any changes in risk factors,
especially if they've been reduced or eliminated.

Once violence hazards are located by analyzing the worksite,
the team or coordinator should design procedures to avoid
them.

Using engineering controls, some hazards can be removed from
the worksite. Barriers can also be placed to shield the worker
from other hazards.

What are some engineering control measures that could be helpful as appropriate to a facility's workplace security analysis?

* Assess any plans for new construction or physical changes to the facility or workplace to eliminate or reduce security hazards.
* Install and regularly maintain alarm systems and other security devices, panic buttons, hand-held alarms or noise devices, cellular phones, and private channel radios where risk is apparent or may be anticipated, and arrange for a reliable response system when an alarm is triggered.
* Provide metal detectors installed or handheld where appropriate to identify guns, knives, or other weapons, according to the recommendations of security consultants.
* Use a closed-circuit video recording for high-risk areas on a 24-hour basis. Public safety is a greater concern than privacy in these situations.
* Place curved mirrors at hallway intersections or concealed areas.
* Enclose nurses' stations, and install deep service counters or bullet-resistant, shatter-proof glass in reception areas, triage, admitting, or client service rooms.
* Provide employee "safe rooms" for use during emergencies.
* Establish "time-out" or seclusion areas with high ceilings without grids for patients acting out and establish separate rooms for criminal patients.
* Provide client or patient waiting rooms designed to maximize comfort and minimize stress.
* Ensure that counseling or patient care rooms have two exits.
* Limit access to staff counseling rooms and treatment rooms controlled by using locked doors.
* Limit the number of pictures, vases, ashtrays, or other items that can be used as weapons.

* Arrange furniture to prevent entrapment of staff. In interview rooms or crisis treatment areas, furniture should be minimal, lightweight, without sharp corners or edges, and/or affixed to the floor.
* Provide lockable and secure bathrooms for staff members separate from patient-client, and visitor facilities.
* Lock all unused doors to limit access, in accordance with local fire codes.
* Install bright, effective lighting indoors and outdoors.
* Replace burned-out lights, broken windows, and locks.
* Keep automobiles, if used in the field, well maintained. Always lock automobiles.

WORK PRACTICE CONTROLS

Some violent incidents can be prevented with the help of administrative and work practice controls, since these controls determine how jobs or tasks are carried out.

What are some administrative and work practice controls that can help to reduce the risk of workplace violence?
* State clearly to patients, clients, and employees that violence is not permitted or tolerated.
* Establish liaison with local police and state prosecutors. Report all incidents of violence. Provide police with physical layouts of facilities to expedite investigations.
* Advise and assist employees, if needed, of company procedures for requesting police assistance or filing charges when assaulted.
* Provide management support during emergencies. Respond promptly to all complaints.
* Set up a trained response team to respond to emergencies.
* Use properly trained security officers, when necessary, to deal with aggressive behavior. Follow written security procedures.

* Ensure adequate and properly trained staff for restraining patients or clients.
* Provide sensitive and timely information to persons waiting in line or in waiting rooms. Adopt measures to decrease waiting time.
* Ensure adequate and qualified staff coverage at all times. Times of greatest risk occur during patient transfers, emergency responses, meal times, and at night. Locales with the greatest risk include admission units and crisis or acute care units. Other risks include admission of patients with a history of violent behavior or gang activity.
* Institute a sign-in procedure with passes for visitors, especially in a newborn nursery or pediatric department. Enforce visitor hours and procedures.
* Establish a list of "restricted visitors" for patients with a history of violence. Copies should be available at security checkpoints, nurses' stations, and visitor sign-in areas. Review and revise visitor check systems, when necessary. Limit information given to outsiders on hospitalized victims of violence.
* Supervise the movement of psychiatric clients and patients throughout the facility.
* Control access to facilities other than waiting rooms, particularly drug storage or pharmacy areas.
* Prohibit employees from working alone in emergency areas or walk-in clinics, particularly at night or when assistance is unavailable. Employees should never enter seclusion rooms alone.
* Establish policies and procedures for secured areas, and emergency evacuations, and for monitoring high-risk patients at night (e.g., open versus locked seclusion).
* Ascertain the behavioral history of new and transferred patients to learn about any past violent or assaultive behaviors. Establish a system such as chart tags, log books, or verbal

census reports to identify patients and clients with assaultive behavior problems, keeping in mind patient confidentiality and worker safety issues. Update as needed.

* Periodically survey the facility to remove tools or possessions left by visitors or maintenance staff which could be used inappropriately by patients.

* Provide staff with identification badges, preferably without last names, to readily verify employment.
Discourage employees from carrying keys, pens, or other items that could be used as weapons.

* Provide staff members with security escorts to parking areas in evening or late hours. Parking areas should be highly visible, well-lighted, and safely accessible to the building.

* Use the "buddy system," especially when personal safety may be threatened. Encourage home health care providers, social service workers, and others to avoid threatening situations. Staff should exercise extra care in elevators, stairwells and unfamiliar residences; immediately leave premises if there is a hazardous situation; or request police escort if needed.

* Develop policies and procedures covering home health care providers, such as contracts on how visits will be conducted, the presence of others in the home during the visits, and the refusal to provide services in a clearly hazardous situation.

* Establish a daily work plan for field staff to keep a designated contact person informed about workers' whereabouts throughout the workday. If an employee does not report in, the contact person should follow up.

* Conduct a comprehensive post-incident evaluation, including psychological as well as medical treatment, for employees who have been subjected to abusive behavior.

RECOVERY

No workplace violence prevention program is complete unless it deals with the aftermath of a violent incident. Employees can suffer directly as violence victims, and indirectly as traumatized witnesses of violence.

Any program that seeks to be effective must include comprehensive treatment and psychological evaluations for every form of assault incident.

There should also be provisions for both short and long-term physical and psychological care. After violence has been experienced, some people may experience debilitating problems.
* Short and long-term psychological trauma
* Fear of returning to work
* Changes in relationships with co-workers and family
* Feelings of incompetence, guilt, powerlessness
* Fear of criticism by supervisors or managers

The post-incident response can include many different kinds of aid to victims. Some of these are:
* Trauma-crisis counseling
* Critical incident stress debriefing
* Employee assistance programs
Who is qualified to provide this type of assistance?
* Certified employee assistance professionals
* Psychologists and psychiatrists
* Clinical nurse specialists
* Social workers
* Outside specialists
* Employee counseling services
* Peer counseling
* Support groups

RECORDKEEPING

In order to identify any inefficiencies or necessary changes, appropriate records need to be kept, and the program needs to be periodically evaluated.

By looking at records, management can:
* Figure out how severe the problems are
* Evaluation hazard control methods
* Determine training needs

One very important record is the OSHA Log of Injury and Illness (OSHA 200).
When regulations require an establishment to keep OSHA logs, entries must be made for any injury that:
* Requires more than first aid
* Is a lost-time injury
* Requires modified duty
* Causes loss of consciousness
* Is caused by assaults

Within 8 hours of any fatality or calamity resulting in 3 or more workers being hospitalized, a report must be made to OSHA (including workplace violence incidents).

Another set of reports that should be kept involves work injury and supervisors' reports for recorded assaults.

These should include a description of:
* The type of assault, (i.e., unprovoked sudden attack or patient-to-patient altercation)
* Who was assaulted
* All other circumstances of the incident

* A description of the environment or location, potential or actual cost, lost time, and the nature of injuries sustained

Also, details about patients who have a history of problem behavior should be recorded on their charts and evaluated.
* Violence
* Drug abuse
* Criminal activity should be recorded on the patient's chart.

Every worker involved in patient care for clients who could be violent, aggressive, or abusive needs to be cognizant of the background and history of these patients. When violent patients are admitted, proper logs and records can aid in risk assessment.

What are some other records that should be documented, maintained and periodically evaluated?
* Minutes of safety meetings
* Records of hazard analyses
* Corrective actions recommended and taken
* Records of all training programs, attendees, and qualifications of trainers

Employers need to evaluate their safety and security measures as a regular procedure of their program.

Program success needs to be evaluated by head managers, as they regularly review the program against each incident.

The program's policies and procedures need to be reevaluated regularly by everyone involved, including managers, supervisors, and employees. Any shortcomings need to be pointed out and steps should be taken to correct the deficiencies.

To be effective, the evaluation should include:
* Establishing a uniform violence reporting system and regular review of reports.
* Reviewing reports and minutes from staff meetings on safety and security issues.
* Analyzing trends and rates in illness/injury or fatalities caused by violence relative to initial or "baseline" rates.
* Measuring improvement based on lowering the frequency and severity of workplace violence.
* Keeping up-to-date records of administrative and work practice changes to prevent workplace violence to evaluate their effectiveness.
* Surveying employees before and after making job or worksite changes or installing security measures or new systems to determine their effectiveness.
* Keeping abreast of new strategies available to deal with violence in the health care and social service fields as these develop.
* Surveying employees who experience hostile situations about the medical treatment they received initially and, again, several weeks afterward, and then several months later.
* Complying with OSHA and state requirements for recording and reporting deaths, injuries, and illnesses.
* Requesting periodic law enforcement or outside consultant review of the worksite for recommendations on improving employee safety.
* Management should share workplace violence prevention program evaluation reports with all employees.

Any changes in the program should be discussed at regular meetings of the safety committee, union representatives, or other employee groups.

OSHA GUIDELINES

NOTICE

Guidelines for Preventing Workplace Violence for Health Care and Social
Services Workers
U.S. Department of Labor
Robert B. Reich, Secretary
Occupational Safety and Health Administration
Joseph A. Dear, Assistant Secretary
OSHA 3148
1996

These guidelines are not a new standard or regulation. They are advisory
in nature, informational in content, and are intended for use by employers
seeking to provide a safe and healthful workplace through effective
workplace violence prevention programs adapted to the needs and
resources of each place of employment. The guidelines are not intended to
address issues related to patient care. The guidelines are performance-
oriented and the implementation of the recommendations will be different
based upon an establishment's hazard analysis.

Violence inflicted upon employees may come from many sources —
i.e., patients, third parties such as robbers or muggers — and may include
co-worker violence. These guidelines address only the violence inflicted
by patients or clients against staff. It is suggested, however, that workplace
violence policies indicate a zero-tolerance for violence of any kind.

The Occupational Safety and Health Act of 1970 (OSH Act)[1]
mandates that, in addition to compliance with hazard-specific standards,
employers have a general duty to provide their employees with a
workplace free from recognized hazards likely to cause death or serious
physical harm. OSHA will rely on Section 5(a) of the OSH Act, the
"General Duty Clause,"[2] for enforcement authority. Employers can be
cited for violating the General Duty Clause if there is a recognized hazard
of workplace violence in their establishments and they do nothing to
prevent or abate it. Failure to implement these guidelines is not in itself a
violation of the General Duty Clause of the OSH Act. OSHA will not cite
employers who have effectively implemented these guidelines.

Further, when Congress passed the OSH Act, it did so based on a
finding that job-related illnesses and injuries were imposing both a
hindrance and a substantial burden upon interstate commerce, "in terms of

lost production, wage loss, medical expenses, and disability compensation payments."[3]

At the same time, Congress was mindful of the fact that workers' compensation systems provided state-specific remedies for job-related injuries and illnesses. Issues on what constitutes a compensable claim and what the rate of compensation should be were left up to the states, their legislatures, and their courts to determine. Congress acknowledged this point in Section 4(b)(4) of the OSH Act, when it stated categorically: " Nothing in this chapter shall be construed to supersede or in any manner affect any workmen's compensation law...."[4] Therefore, these non-mandatory guidelines should not be viewed as enlarging or diminishing the scope of work-related injuries and are intended for use in any state and without regard to whether the injuries or fatalities, if any, are later deemed to be compensable.

ACKNOWLEDGEMENTS

Many persons, including health care, social services, and employee assistance experts; researchers, educators; unions, and other stakeholders; OSHA professionals; and the National Institute for Occupational Safety and Health (NIOSH) contributed to these guidelines.

Also, several states have developed relevant standards or recommendations, such as the California OSHA (CAL/OSHA), CAL/OSHA Guidelines for Workplace Security, and Guidelines for Security and Safety of Health Care and Community Service Workers; the Joint Commission on Accreditation of Healthcare Organizations, 1995 Accreditation Manual for Hospitals; Metropolitan Chicago Healthcare Council, Guidelines for Dealing with Violence in Health Care; New Jersey Public Employees Occupational Safety and Health (PEOSH), Guidelines on Measures and Safeguards in Dealing with Violent or Aggressive Behavior in Public Sector Health Care Facilities; and the State of Washington Department of Labor and Industries, Violence in Washington Workplaces, and Study of Assaults on Staff in Washington State Psychiatric Hospitals. Information is available from these and other agencies to assist employers.

INTRODUCTION

For many years, health care and social service workers have faced a significant risk of job-related violence. Assaults represent a serious safety and health hazard for these industries, and violence against their employees continues to increase.

OSHA's new violence prevention guidelines provide the agency's recommendations for reducing workplace violence developed following a careful review of workplace violence studies, public and private violence prevention programs, and consultations with and input from stakeholders.

OSHA encourages employers to establish violence prevention programs and to track their progress in reducing work-related assaults. Although not every incident can be prevented, many can, and the severity of injuries sustained by employees reduced. Adopting practical measures such as those outlined here can significantly reduce this serious threat to worker safety.

OSHA's Commitment

The publication and distribution of these guidelines is OSHA's first step in assisting health care and social service employers and providers in preventing workplace violence. OSHA plans to conduct a coordinated effort consisting of research, information, training, cooperative programs, and appropriate enforcement to accomplish this goal.

The guidelines are not a new standard or regulation. They are advisory in nature, informational in content, and intended for use by employers in providing a safe and healthful workplace through effective violence prevention programs, adapted to the needs and resources of each place of employment.

Extent of Problem

Today, more assaults occur in the health care and social services industries than in any other. For example, Bureau of Labor Statistics (BLS) data for 1993 showed health care and social service workers having the highest incidence of assault injuries (BLS, 1993). Almost two-thirds of the nonfatal assaults occurred in nursing homes, hospitals, and establishments providing residential care and other social services (Toscano and Weber, 1995).

Assaults against workers in the health professions are not new. According to one study (Goodman et al., 1994), between 1980 and 1990, 106 occupational violence-related deaths occurred among the following health care workers: 27 pharmacists, 26 physicians, 18 registered nurses, 17 nurses' aides, and 18 health care workers in other occupational categories. Using the National Traumatic Occupational Fatality database, the study reported that between 1983 and 1989, there were 69 registered nurses killed at work. Homicide was the leading cause of traumatic occupational death among employees in nursing homes and personal care facilities.

A 1989 report (Carmel and Hunter) found that the nursing staff at a psychiatric hospital sustained 16 assaults per 100 employees per year. This rate, which includes any assault-related injuries, compares with 8.3 injuries of all types per 100 full-time workers in all industries and 14.2 per 100 full-time workers in the construction industry (BLS, 1991). Of 121 psychiatric hospital workers sustaining 134 injuries, 43 percent involved lost time from work with 13 percent of those injured missing more than 21 days from work.

Of greater concern is the likely underreporting of violence and a persistent perception within the health care industry that assaults are part of the job. Underreporting may reflect a lack of institutional reporting policies, employee beliefs that reporting will not benefit them, or employee fears that employers may deem assaults the result of employee negligence or poor job performance.

Risk Factors

Health care and social service workers face an increased risk of work-related assaults stemming from several factors, including:

- The prevalence of handguns and other weapons as high as 25 percent[5] — among patients, their families, or friends. The increasing use of hospitals by police and the criminal justice systems for criminal holds and the care of acutely disturbed, violent individuals.
- The increasing number of acute and chronically mentally ill patients now being released from hospitals without followup care, who now have the right to refuse medicine and who can no longer be hospitalized involuntarily unless they pose an immediate threat to themselves or others.
- The availability of drugs or money at hospitals, clinics, and pharmacies, making them likely robbery targets.
- Situational and circumstantial factors such as unrestricted movement of the public in clinics and hospitals; the increasing presence of gang members, drug or alcohol abusers, trauma patients, or distraught family members; long waits in emergency or clinic areas, leading to client frustration over an inability to obtain needed services promptly.
- Low staffing levels during times of specific increased activity such as meal times, visiting times, and when staff are transporting patients.
- Isolated work with clients during examinations or treatment.

- Solo work, often in remote locations, particularly in high-crime settings, with no back-up or means of obtaining assistance, such as communication devices or alarm systems.
- Lack of training of staff in recognizing and managing escalating hostile and assaultive behavior.
- Poorly lighted parking areas.

Overview of Guidelines

In January 1989, OSHA published voluntary, generic safety and health program management guidelines for all employers to use as a foundation for their safety and health programs, which can include a workplace violence prevention program.[6] OSHA's violence prevention guidelines build on the 1989 generic guidelines by identifying common risk factors and describing some feasible solutions. Although not exhaustive, the new workplace violence guidelines include policy recommendations and practical corrective methods to help prevent and mitigate the effects of workplace violence.

The goal is to eliminate or reduce worker exposure to conditions that lead to death or injury from violence by implementing effective security devices and administrative work practices, among other control measures.

The guidelines cover a broad spectrum of workers who provide health care and social services in psychiatric facilities, hospital emergency departments, community mental health clinics, drug abuse treatment clinics, pharmacies, community care facilities, and long-term care facilities. They include physicians, registered nurses, pharmacists, nurse practitioners, physicians' assistants, nurses' aides, therapists, technicians, public health nurses, home health care workers, social/welfare workers, and emergency medical care personnel. Further, the guidelines may be useful in reducing risks for ancillary personnel such as maintenance, dietary, clerical, and security staff employed in the health care and social services industries.

VIOLENCE PREVENTION PROGRAM ELEMENTS

There are four main components to any effective safety and health program that also apply to preventing workplace violence: (1) management commitment and employee involvement, (2) worksite analysis, (3) hazard prevention and control, and (4) safety and health training.

Management Commitment and Employee Involvement

Management commitment and employee involvement are complementary and essential elements of an effective safety and health program. To ensure an effective program, management and front-line employees must work together, perhaps through a team or committee approach. If employers opt for this strategy, they must be careful to comply with the applicable provisions of the National Labor Relations Act.[2]

Management commitment, including the endorsement and visible involvement of top management, provides the motivation and resources to deal effectively with workplace violence, and should include the following:

- Demonstrated organizational concern for employee emotional and physical safety and health.
- Equal commitment to worker safety and health and patient/client safety.
- Assigned responsibility for the various aspects of the workplace violence prevention program to ensure that all managers, supervisors, and employees understand their obligations.
- Appropriate allocation of authority and resources to all responsible parties.
- A system of accountability for involved managers, supervisors, and employees.
- A comprehensive program of medical and psychological counseling and debriefing for employees experiencing or witnessing assaults and other violent incidents.
- Commitment to support and implement appropriate recommendations from safety and health committees.

Employee involvement and feedback enable workers to develop and express their own commitment to safety and health and provide useful information to design, implement, and evaluate the program.

Employee involvement should include the following:

- Understanding and complying with the workplace violence prevention program and other safety and security measures.
- Participation in an employee complaint or suggestion procedure covering safety and security concerns.
- Prompt and accurate reporting of violent incidents.

- Participation on safety and health committees or teams that receive reports of violent incidents or security problems, make facility inspections, and respond with recommendations for corrective strategies.
- Taking part in a continuing education program that covers techniques to recognize escalating agitation, assaultive behavior, or criminal intent, and discusses appropriate responses.

Written program. A written program for job safety and security, incorporated into the organization's overall safety and health program, offers an effective approach for larger organizations. In smaller establishments, the program need not be written or heavily documented to be satisfactory. What is needed are clear goals and objectives to prevent workplace violence suitable for the size and complexity of the workplace operation and adaptable to specific situations in each establishment.

The prevention program and startup date must be communicated to all employees. At a minimum, workplace violence prevention programs should do the following:

- Create and disseminate a clear policy of zero- tolerance for workplace violence, verbal and nonverbal threats, and related actions. Managers, supervisors, co-workers, clients, patients, and visitors must be advised of this policy.
- Ensure that no reprisals are taken against an employee who reports or experiences workplace violence.[8]
- Encourage employees to promptly report incidents and to suggest ways to reduce or eliminate risks. Require records of incidents to assess risk and to measure progress.
- Outline a comprehensive plan for maintaining security in the workplace, which includes establishing a liaison with law enforcement representatives and others who can help identify ways to prevent and mitigate workplace violence.
- Assign responsibility and authority for the program to individuals or teams with appropriate training and skills. The written plan should ensure that there are adequate resources available for this effort and that the team or responsible individuals develop expertise on workplace violence prevention in health care and social services.

- Affirm management commitment to a worker- supportive environment that places as much importance on employee safety and health as on serving the patient or client.
- Set up a company briefing as part of the initial effort to address such issues as preserving safety, supporting affected employees, and facilitating recovery.

Worksite Analysis

Worksite analysis involves a step-by-step, common-sense look at the workplace to find existing or potential hazards for workplace violence. This entails reviewing specific procedures or operations that contribute to hazards and specific locales where hazards may develop.

A "Threat Assessment Team," "Patient Assault Team," similar task force, or coordinator may assess the vulnerability to workplace violence and determine the appropriate preventive actions to be taken. Implementing the workplace violence prevention program then may be assigned to this group. The team should include representatives from senior management, operations, employee assistance, security, occupational safety and health, legal, and human resources staff.

The team or coordinator can review injury and illness records and workers' compensation claims to identify patterns of assaults that could be prevented by workplace adaptation, procedural changes, or employee training. As the team or coordinator identifies appropriate controls, these should be instituted.

The recommended program for worksite analysis includes, but is not limited to, analyzing and tracking records, monitoring trends and analyzing incidents, screening surveys, and analyzing workplace security.

Records analysis and tracking. This activity should include reviewing medical, safety, workers' compensation and insurance records including the OSHA 200 log, if required to pinpoint instances of workplace violence. Scan unit logs and employee and police reports of incidents or near-incidents of assaultive behavior to identify and analyze trends in assaults relative to particular departments, units, job titles, unit activities, work stations, and/or time of day. Tabulate these data to target the frequency and severity of incidents to establish a baseline for measuring improvement.

Monitoring trends and analyzing incidents. Contacting similar local businesses, trade associations, and community and civic groups is one way to learn about their experiences with workplace violence and to help identify trends. Use several years of data, if possible, to trace trends of injuries and incidents of actual or potential workplace violence.

Screening surveys. One important screening tool is to give employees a questionnaire or survey to get their ideas on the potential for violent incidents and to identify or confirm the need for improved security measures. Detailed baseline screening surveys can help pinpoint tasks that put employees at risk. Periodic surveys conducted at least annually or whenever operations change or incidents of workplace violence occur help identify new or previously unnoticed risk factors and deficiencies or failures in work practices, procedures, or controls. Also, the surveys help assess the effects of changes in the work processes (see Appendix A for a sample survey used in the State of Washington). The periodic review process should also include feedback and followup.

Independent reviewers, such as safety and health professionals, law enforcement or security specialists, insurance safety auditors, and other qualified persons may offer advice to strengthen programs. These experts also can provide fresh perspectives to improve a violence prevention program.

Workplace security analysis. The team or coordinator should periodically inspect the workplace and evaluate employee tasks to identify hazards, conditions, operations, and situations that could lead to violence. To find areas requiring further evaluation, the team or coordinator should do the following:

- Analyze incidents, including the characteristics of assailants and victims, an account of what happened before and during the incident, and the relevant details of the situation and its outcome. When possible, obtain police reports and recommendations.
- Identify jobs or locations with the greatest risk of violence as well as processes and procedures that put employees at risk of assault, including how often and when.
- Note high-risk factors such as types of clients or patients (e.g., psychiatric conditions or patients disoriented by drugs, alcohol, or stress); physical risk factors of the building; isolated locations/job activities; lighting problems; lack of phones and other communication devices, areas of easy, unsecured access; and areas with previous security problems. (See sample checklist for assessing hazards in Appendix B.)
- Evaluate the effectiveness of existing security measures, including engineering control measures. Determine if risk factors have been reduced or eliminated, and take appropriate action.

Hazard Prevention and Control

After hazards of violence are identified through the systematic worksite analysis, the next step is to design measures through engineering or administrative and work practices to prevent or control these hazards. If violence does occur, post-incidence response can be an important tool in preventing future incidents.

Engineering controls and workplace adaptation. Engineering controls, for example, remove the hazard from the workplace or create a barrier between the worker and the hazard. There are several measures that can effectively prevent or control workplace hazards, such as those actions presented in the following paragraphs. The selection of any measure, of course, should be based upon the hazards identified in the workplace security analysis of each facility.

- Assess any plans for new construction or physical changes to the facility or workplace to eliminate or reduce security hazards.
- Install and regularly maintain alarm systems and other security devices, panic buttons, hand-held alarms or noise devices, cellular phones, and private channel radios where risk is apparent or may be anticipated, and arrange for a reliable response system when an alarm is triggered.
- Provide metal detectors installed or hand-held, where appropriate to identify guns, knives, or other weapons, according to the recommendations of security consultants.
- Use a closed-circuit video recording for high- risk areas on a 24-hour basis. Public safety is a greater concern than privacy in these situations.
- Place curved mirrors at hallway intersections or concealed areas.
- Enclose nurses' stations, and install deep service counters or bullet-resistant, shatter-proof glass in reception areas, triage, admitting, or client service rooms.
- Provide employee "safe rooms" for use during emergencies.
- Establish "time-out" or seclusion areas with high ceilings without grids for patients acting out and establish separate rooms for criminal patients.
- Provide client or patient waiting rooms designed to maximize comfort and minimize stress.
- Ensure that counseling or patient care rooms have two exits.
- Limit access to staff counseling rooms and treatment rooms controlled by using locked doors.

- Arrange furniture to prevent entrapment of staff. In interview rooms or crisis treatment areas, furniture should be minimal, lightweight, without sharp corners or edges, and/or affixed to the floor. Limit the number of pictures, vases, ashtrays, or other items that can be used as weapons.
- Provide lockable and secure bathrooms for staff members separate from patient-client and visitor facilities.
- Lock all unused doors to limit access, in accordance with local fire codes.
- Install bright, effective lighting indoors and outdoors.
- Replace burned-out lights, broken windows, and locks.
- Keep aut\omobiles, if used in the field, well- maintained. Always lock automobiles.

Administrative and work practice controls. Administrative and work practice controls affect the way jobs or tasks are performed. The following examples illustrate how changes in work practices and administrative procedures can help prevent violent incidents.

- State clearly to patients, clients, and employees that violence is not permitted or tolerated.
- Establish liaison with local police and state prosecutors. Report all incidents of violence. Provide police with physical layouts of facilities to expedite investigations.
- Require employees to report all assaults or threats to a supervisor or manager (e.g., can be confidential interview). Keep log books and reports of such incidents to help in determining any necessary actions to prevent further occurrences.
- Advise and assist employees, if needed, of company procedures for requesting police assistance or filing charges when assaulted.
- Provide management support during emergencies. Respond promptly to all complaints.
- Set up a trained response team to respond to emergencies.
- Use properly trained security officers, when necessary, to deal with aggressive behavior. Follow written security procedures.
- Ensure adequate and properly trained staff for restraining patients or clients.
- Provide sensitive and timely information to persons waiting in line or in waiting rooms. Adopt measures to decrease waiting time.

- Ensure adequate and qualified staff coverage at all times. Times of greatest risk occur during patient transfers, emergency responses, meal times, and at night. Locales with the greatest risk include admission units and crisis or acute care units. Other risks include admission of patients with a history of violent behavior or gang activity.
- Institute a sign-in procedure with passes for visitors, especially in a newborn nursery or pediatric department. Enforce visitor hours and procedures.
- Establish a list of "restricted visitors" for patients with a history of violence. Copies should be available at security checkpoints, nurses' stations, and visitor sign-in areas. Review and revise visitor check systems, when necessary. Limit information given to outsiders on hospitalized victims of violence.
- Supervise the movement of psychiatric clients and patients throughout the facility.
- Control access to facilities other than waiting rooms, particularly drug storage or pharmacy areas.
- Prohibit employees from working alone in emergency areas or walk-in clinics, particularly at night or when assistance is unavailable. Employees should never enter seclusion rooms alone.
- Establish policies and procedures for secured areas, and emergency evacuations, and for monitoring high-risk patients at night (e.g., open versus locked seclusion).
- Ascertain the behavioral history of new and transferred patients to learn about any past violent or assaultive behaviors. Establish a system such as chart tags, log books, or verbal census reports to identify patients and clients with assaultive behavior problems, keeping in mind patient confidentiality and worker safety issues. Update as needed.
- Treat and/or interview aggressive or agitated clients in relatively open areas that still maintain privacy and confidentiality (e.g., rooms with removable partitions).
- Use case management conferences with co- workers and supervisors to discuss ways to effectively treat potentially violent patients.
- Prepare contingency plans to treat clients who are "acting out" or making verbal or physical attacks or threats. Consider using certified employee assistance professionals (CEAPs) or in-house

social service or occupational health service staff to help diffuse patient or client anger.

- Transfer assaultive clients to "acute care units," "criminal units," or other more restrictive settings.
- Make sure that nurses and/or physicians are not alone when performing intimate physical examinations of patients.
- Discourage employees from wearing jewelry to help prevent possible strangulation in confrontational situations. Community workers should carry only required identification and money.
- Periodically survey the facility to remove tools or possessions left by visitors or maintenance staff which could be used inappropriately by patients.
- Provide staff with identification badges, preferably without last names, to readily verify employment.
- Discourage employees from carrying keys, pens, or other items that could be used as weapons.
- Provide staff members with security escorts to parking areas in evening or late hours. Parking areas should be highly visible, well-lighted, and safely accessible to the building.
- Use the "buddy system," especially when personal safety may be threatened. Encourage home health care providers, social service workers, and others to avoid threatening situations. Staff should exercise extra care in elevators, stairwells and unfamiliar residences; immediately leave premises if there is a hazardous situation; or request police escort if needed.
- Develop policies and procedures covering home health care providers, such as contracts on how visits will be conducted, the presence of others in the home during the visits, and the refusal to provide services in a clearly hazardous situation.
- Establish a daily work plan for field staff to keep a designated contact person informed about workers' whereabouts throughout the workday. If an employee does not report in, the contact person should followup.
- Conduct a comprehensive post-incident evaluation, including psychological as well as medical treatment, for employees who have been subjected to abusive behavior.

Post-incident response. Post-incident response and evaluation are essential to an effective violence prevention program. All workplace violence programs should provide comprehensive treatment for victimized employees and employees who may be traumatized by witnessing a workplace violence incident. Injured staff should receive prompt treatment and psychological evaluation whenever an assault takes place, regardless of severity. (See sample hospital policy in Appendix C). Transportation of the injured to medical care should be provided if care is not available on-site.

Victims of workplace violence suffer a variety of consequences in addition to their actual physical injuries. These include short and long-term psychological trauma, fear of returning to work, changes in relationships with co-workers and family, feelings of incompetence, guilt, powerlessness, and fear of criticism by supervisors or managers. Consequently, a strong followup program for these employees will not only help them to deal with these problems but also to help prepare them to confront or prevent future incidents of violence (Flannery, 1991; 1993; 1995).

There are several types of assistance that can be incorporated into the post-incident response. For example, trauma-crisis counseling, critical incident stress debriefing, or employee assistance programs may be provided to assist victims. Certified employee assistance professionals, psychologists, psychiatrists, clinical nurse specialists, or social workers could provide this counseling, or the employer can refer staff victims to an outside specialist. In addition, an employee counseling service, peer counseling, or support groups may be established.

In any case, counselors must be well trained and have a good understanding of the issues and consequences of assaults and other aggressive, violent behavior. Appropriate and promptly rendered post-incident debriefings and counseling reduce acute psychological trauma and general stress levels among victims and witnesses. In addition, such counseling educates staff about workplace violence and positively influences workplace and organizational cultural norms to reduce trauma associated with future incidents.

Training and Education

Training and education ensure that all staff are aware of potential security hazards and how to protect themselves and their co-workers through established policies and procedures.

All employees. Every employee should understand the concept of "Universal Precautions for Violence," i.e., that violence should be expected but can be avoided or mitigated through preparation. Staff should be instructed to limit physical interventions in workplace altercations whenever possible, unless there are adequate numbers of staff or emergency response teams and security personnel available. Frequent training also can improve the likelihood of avoiding assault (Carmel and Hunter, 1990).

Employees who may face safety and security hazards should receive formal instruction on the specific hazards associated with the unit or job and facility. This includes information on the types of injuries or problems identified in the facility and the methods to control the specific hazards.

The training program should involve all employees, including supervisors and managers. New and reassigned employees should receive an initial orientation prior to being assigned their job duties. Visiting staff, such as physicians, should receive the same training as permanent staff. Qualified trainers should instruct at the comprehension level appropriate for the staff. Effective training programs should involve role playing, simulations, and drills.

Topics may include Management of Assaultive Behavior; Professional Assault Response Training; police assault avoidance programs, or personal safety training such as awareness, avoidance, and how to prevent assaults. A combination of training may be used depending on the severity of the risk.

Required training should be provided to employees annually. In large institutions, refresher programs may be needed more frequently (monthly or quarterly) to effectively reach and inform all employees.

The training should cover topics such as the following:

- The workplace violence prevention policy.
- Risk factors that cause or contribute to assaults.
- Early recognition of escalating behavior or recognition of warning signs or situations that may lead to assaults.
- Ways of preventing or diffusing volatile situations or aggressive behavior, managing anger, and appropriately using medications as chemical restraints.
- Information on multicultural diversity to develop sensitivity to racial and ethnic issues and differences.
- A standard response action plan for violent situations, including availability of assistance, response to alarm systems, and communication procedures.
- How to deal with hostile persons other than patients and clients, such as relatives and visitors.
- Progressive behavior control methods and safe methods of restraint application or escape.

- The location and operation of safety devices such as alarm systems, along with the required maintenance schedules and procedures.
- Ways to protect oneself and coworkers, including use of the "buddy system."
- Policies and procedures for reporting and recordkeeping.
- Policies and procedures for obtaining medical care, counseling, workers' compensation, or legal assistance after a violent episode or injury.

Supervisors, managers, and security personnel. Supervisors and managers should ensure that employees are not placed in assignments that compromise safety and should encourage employees to report incidents. Employees and supervisors should be trained to behave compassionately towards coworkers when an incident occurs.

They should learn how to reduce security hazards and ensure that employees receive appropriate training. Following training, supervisors and managers should be able to recognize a potentially hazardous situation and to make any necessary changes in the physical plant, patient care treatment program, and staffing policy and procedures to reduce or eliminate the hazards.

Security personnel need specific training from the hospital or clinic, including the psychological components of handling aggressive and abusive clients, types of disorders, and ways to handle aggression and defuse hostile situations.

The training program should also include an evaluation. The content, methods, and frequency of training should be reviewed and evaluated annually by the team or coordinator responsible for implementation. Program evaluation may involve supervisor and/or employee interviews, testing and observing, and/or reviewing reports of behavior of individuals in threatening situations.

RECORDKEEPING AND EVALUATION OF THE PROGRAM

Recordkeeping and evaluation of the violence prevention program are necessary to determine overall effectiveness and identify any deficiencies or changes that should be made.

Recordkeeping

Recordkeeping is essential to the success of a workplace violence prevention program. Good records help employers determine the severity of the problem, evaluate methods of hazard control, and identify training needs. Records can be especially useful to large organizations and for members of a business group or trade association who "pool" data. Records of injuries, illnesses, accidents, assaults, hazards, corrective actions, patient histories, and training, among others, can help identify problems and solutions for an effective program.

The following records are important:

- OSHA Log of Injury and Illness (OSHA 200). OSHA regulations require entry on the Injury and Illness Log of any injury that requires more than first aid, is a lost-time injury, requires modified duty, or causes loss of consciousness.[9] (This applies only to establishments required to keep OSHA logs.) Injuries caused by assaults, which are otherwise recordable, also must be entered on the log. A fatality or catastrophe that results in the hospitalization of 3 or more employees must be reported to OSHA within 8 hours. This includes those resulting from workplace violence and applies to all establishments.

- Medical reports of work injury and supervisors' reports for each recorded assault should be kept.These records should describe the type of assault, i.e., unprovoked sudden attack or patient-to-patient altercation; who was assaulted; and all other circumstances of the incident. The records should include a description of the environment or location, potential or actual cost, lost time, and the nature of injuries sustained.

- Incidents of abuse, verbal attacks or aggressive behavior which may be threatening to the worker but do not result in injury, such as pushing or shouting and acts of aggression towards other clients should be recorded, perhaps as part of an assaultive incident report. These reports should be evaluated routinely by the affected department. (See sample incident forms in Appendix D).

- Information on patients with a history of past violence, drug abuse, or criminal activity should be recorded on the patient's chart. All staff who care for a potentially aggressive, abusive, or violent client should be aware of their background and history.Admission of violent clients should be logged to help determine potential risks.

- Minutes of safety meetings, records of hazard analyses, and corrective actions recommended and taken should be documented.

- Records of all training programs, attendees, and qualifications of trainers should be maintained.

Evaluation

As part of their overall program, employers should evaluate their safety and security measures. Top management should review the program regularly, and with each incident, to evaluate program success. Responsible parties (managers, supervisors, and employees) should collectively reevaluate policies and procedures on a regular basis. Deficiencies should be identified and corrective action taken.

An evaluation program should involve the following:

- Establishing a uniform violence reporting system and regular review of reports.
- Reviewing reports and minutes from staff meetings on safety and security issues.
- Analyzing trends and rates in illness/injury or fatalities caused by violence relative to initial or "baseline" rates.
- Measuring improvement based on lowering the frequency and severity of workplace violence.
- Keeping up-to-date records of administrative and work practice changes to prevent workplace violence to evaluate their effectiveness.
- Surveying employees before and after making job or worksite changes or installing security measures or new systems to determine their effectiveness.
- Keeping abreast of new strategies available to deal with violence in the health care and social service fields as these develop.
- Surveying employees who experience hostile situations about the medical treatment they received initially and, again, several weeks afterward, and then several months later.
- Complying with OSHA and state requirements for recording and reporting deaths, injuries, and illnesses.
- Requesting periodic law enforcement or outside consultant review of the worksite for recommendations on improving employee safety.

Management should share workplace violence prevention program evaluation reports with all employees. Any changes in the program should be discussed at regular meetings of the safety committee, union representatives, or other employee groups.

Sources of Assistance

Employers who would like assistance in implementing an appropriate workplace violence prevention program can turn to the OSHA Consultation service provided in their state. Primarily targeted at smaller companies, the consultation service is provided at no charge to the employer and is independent of OSHA's enforcement activity. (See Appendix E.)

OSHA's efforts to assist employers combat workplace violence are complemented by those of NIOSH (1-800-35-NIOSH) and public safety officials, trade associations, unions, insurers, human resource, and employee assistance professionals as well as other interested groups. Employers and employees may contact these groups for additional advice and information.

CONCLUSION

OSHA recognizes the importance of effective safety and health program management in providing safe and healthful workplaces. In fact, OSHA's consultation services help employers establish and maintain safe and healthful workplaces, and the agency's Voluntary Protection Programs were specifically established to recognize worksites with exemplary safety and health programs. (See Appendix E.) Effective safety and health programs are known to improve both morale and productivity and reduce workers' compensation costs.

OSHA's violence prevention guidelines are an essential component to workplace safety and health programs. OSHA believes that the performance-oriented approach of the guidelines provides employers with flexibility in their efforts to maintain safe and healthful working conditions.

---

[1] Public Law 91-596, December 29, 1970; and as amended by P. L. 101-552, Section 3101, November 5, 1990.

[2] "Each employer shall furnish to each of his employees employment and a place of employment which are free from recognized hazards that are causing or are likely to cause death or serious physical harm to his

employees. "

[3] 29 U. S. C. 651(a).

[4] 29 U. S. C. 653(b)(4).

[5] According to a 1989 report (Wasserberger), 25 percent of major trauma patients treated in the emergency room carried weapons. Attacks in emergency rooms in gang- related shootings as well as planned escapes from police custody have been documented in hospitals. A 1991 report (Goetz et al.) also found that 17. 3 percent of psychiatric patients searched were carrying weapons.

[6] OSHA's Safety and Health Program Management Guidelines (Fed Reg 54 (16):3904-3916, January 26, 1989), provide for comprehensive safety and health programs containing these major elements. Employers with such programs can include workplace violence prevention efforts in that context.

[7] Title 29 U. S. C. , Section 158(a)(2).

[8] Section 11(c)(1) of the OSH Act, which also applies to protected activity involving the hazard of workplace violence as it does for other health and safety matters: "No person shall discharge or in any manner discriminate against any employee because such employee has filed any complaint or instituted or caused to be instituted any proceeding under or related to this Act or has testified or is about to testify in any such proceeding or because of the exercise by such employee on behalf of himself or others of any right afforded by this Act. "

[9] The Occupational Safety and Health Act and recordkeeping regulations in Title 29 Code of Federal Regulations (CFR), Part 1904 provide specific recording requirements that comprise the framework of the occupational safety and health recording system (BLS, 1986a). BLS has issued guidelines that provide official Agency interpretations concerning the recordkeeping and reporting of occupational injuries and illnesses (BLS, 1986b).

CD Order Form for CD-ROM Training Programs from UniversityOfHealthCare/UniversityOfBusiness

Title Name	Price	Quantity	Total
Advanced Sales Skills Certificate Program	$299.95		
Advanced Sales Skills Certificate Program Manual and CD	$319.95		
Advanced Sales Skills Program Library Edition	$399.95		
Agent GCP and the Bloody Consent Form	$349.95		
Agent GCP and the Bloody Consent Form Library Edition	$499.95		
Agent GCP and the Bloody Consent Form Manual and CD	$379.95		
Agent GXP FDA Part 11	$199.95		
Agent GXP FDA Part 11 Library Edition	$299.95		
Agent GXP FDA Part 11 Manual and CD	$229.95		
Bioterrorism Anthrax	$49.95		
Bioterrorism Anthrax Library Edition	$99.95		
Bioterrorism Anthrax Manual and CD	$59.95		
Bioterrorism Botulinum	$49.95		
Bioterrorism Botulinum Library Edition	$99.95		
Bioterrorism Botulinum Manual and CD	$59.95		
Bioterrorism Certificate Program	$299.95		
Bioterrorism Certificate Program Manual and CD	$319.95		
Bioterrorism Hemorrhagic Viruses	$49.95		
Bioterrorism Hemorrhagic Viruses Library Edition	$99.95		
Bioterrorism Hemorrhagic Viruses Manual and CD	$59.95		
Bioterrorism Plague	$49.95		
Bioterrorism Plague Library Edition	$99.95		
Bioterrorism Plague Manual and CD	$59.95		
Bioterrorism Program Library Edition	$399.95		
Bioterrorism Radiation	$49.95		
Bioterrorism Radiation Library Edition	$99.95		
Bioterrorism Radiation Manual and CD	$59.95		
Bioterrorism Smallpox	$49.95		
Bioterrorism Smallpox Library Edition	$99.95		
Bioterrorism Smallpox Manual and CD	$59.95		
Bioterrorism Tularemia	$49.95		
Bioterrorism Tularemia Library Edition	$99.95		
Bioterrorism Tularemia Manual and CD	$59.95		
Customer and Patient Care	$49.95		
Customer and Patient Care Library Edition	$99.95		
Customer and Patient Care Manual and CD	$59.95		
Customer Care in Healthcare Certificate Program	$199.95		
Customer Care in Healthcare Certificate Program Manual and CD	$219.95		
Customer Care in Healthcare Program Library Edition	$299.95		
GMP Training Package	$449.95		
GMP Training Package Library Edition	$599.95		
GMP Training Package Manual and CD	$499.95		
Handling Difficult People	$49.95		

Title Name	Price	Quantity	Total
Handling Difficult People Library Edition	$99.95		
Handling Difficult People Manual and CD	$59.95		
Healthcare Fraud and Abuse Introduction	$49.95		
Healthcare Fraud and Abuse Introduction Library Edition	$99.95		
Healthcare Fraud and Abuse Introduction Manual and CD	$59.95		
HIPAA 1 Overview	$49.95		
HIPAA 1 Overview Library Edition	$99.95		
HIPAA 1 Overview Manual and CD	$59.95		
HIPAA 2 Business Associates and Covered Entities	$49.95		
HIPAA 2 Business Associates and Covered Entities Library Edition	$99.95		
HIPAA 2 Business Associates and Covered Entities Manual and CD	$59.95		
HIPAA 3A Privacy Uses and Disclosures	$49.95		
HIPAA 3A Privacy Uses and Disclosures Library Edition	$99.95		
HIPAA 3A Privacy Uses and Disclosures Manual and CD	$59.95		
HIPAA 3B Psychotherapy and Country Doctors	$29.95		
HIPAA 3B Psychotherapy and Country Doctors Library Edition	$79.95		
HIPAA 3B Psychotherapy and Country Doctors Manual and CD	$39.95		
HIPAA 3C Marketing	$49.95		
HIPAA 3C Marketing Library Edition	$99.95		
HIPAA 3C Marketing Manual and CD	$59.95		
HIPAA 3D Notice of Privacy Practices	$49.95		
HIPAA 3D Notice of Privacy Practices Library Edition	$99.95		
HIPAA 3D Notice of Privacy Practices Manual and CD	$59.95		
HIPAA Focused Training 1 Overview	$49.95		
HIPAA Focused Training 1 Overview Library Edition	$99.95		
HIPAA Focused Training 1 Overview Manual and CD	$59.95		
HIPAA Focused Training 2 Business Associates and Covered Entities	$49.95		
HIPAA Focused Training 2 Business Associates and Covered Entities Library Edition	$99.95		
HIPAA Focused Training 2 Business Associates and Covered Entities Manual and CD	$59.95		
HIPAA Focused Training 3A Privacy Uses and Disclosures	$49.95		
HIPAA Focused Training 3A Privacy Uses and Disclosures Library Edition	$99.95		
HIPAA Focused Training 3A Privacy Uses and Disclosures Manual and CD	$59.95		
HIPAA Focused Training 3B Psychotherapy and Country Doctors	$29.95		
HIPAA Focused Training 3B Psychotherapy and Country Doctors Library Edition	$79.95		
HIPAA Focused Training 3B Psychotherapy and Country Doctors Manual and CD	$39.95		
HIPAA Focused Training 3C Marketing	$49.95		
HIPAA Focused Training 3C Marketing Library Edition	$99.95		
HIPAA Focused Training 3C Marketing Manual and CD	$59.95		
HIPAA Focused Training 3D Notice of Privacy Practices	$49.95		
HIPAA Focused Training 3D Notice of Privacy Practices Library Edition	$99.95		
HIPAA Focused Training 3D Notice of Privacy Practices Manual and CD	$59.95		
HIPAA Focused Training 4A Data and Computer Security	$49.95		
HIPAA Focused Training 4A Data and Computer Security Library Edition	$99.95		
HIPAA Focused Training 4A Data and Computer Security Manual and CD	$59.95		

Title Name	Price	Quantity	Total
HIPAA Privacy Certificate Program	$299.95		
HIPAA Privacy Certificate Program Manual and CD	$339.95		
HIPAA Privacy Compliance Planning	$49.95		
HIPAA Privacy Compliance Planning Library Edition	$99.95		
HIPAA Privacy Compliance Planning Manual and CD	$59.95		
HIPAA Privacy Program Library Edition	$399.95		
Internet Searches	$74.95		
Internet Searches Library Edition	$124.95		
Internet Searches Manual and CD	$84.95		
Laugh and Learn Pharmaceutical Sales Code	$49.95		
Laugh and Learn Pharmaceutical Sales Code Library Edition	$99.95		
Laugh and Learn Pharmaceutical Sales Code Manual and CD	$59.95		
Laugh and Learn Sales Letters 1	$49.95		
Laugh and Learn Sales Letters 1 Library Edition	$99.95		
Laugh and Learn Sales Letters 1 Manual and CD	$59.95		
Laugh and Learn Sales Territory Management	$49.95		
Laugh and Learn Sales Territory Management Library Edition	$99.95		
Laugh and Learn Sales Territory Management Manual and CD	$59.95		
Laugh and Learn Sales Time Management	$49.95		
Laugh and Learn Sales Time Management Library Edition	$99.95		
Laugh and Learn Sales Time Management Manual and CD	$59.95		
Multidrug Resistant Tuberculosis	$49.95		
Multidrug Resistant Tuberculosis Library Edition	$99.95		
Multidrug Resistant Tuberculosis Manual and CD	$59.95		
OSHA Bloodborne Pathogens	$49.95		
OSHA Bloodborne Pathogens Library Edition	$99.95		
OSHA Bloodborne Pathogens Manual and CD	$59.95		
OSHA Carpal Tunnel Syndrome	$49.95		
OSHA Carpal Tunnel Syndrome Library Edition	$99.95		
OSHA Carpal Tunnel Syndrome Manual and CD	$59.95		
OSHA Computer Related Illness	$49.95		
OSHA Computer Related Illness Library Edition	$99.95		
OSHA Computer Related Illness Manual and CD	$59.95		
OSHA Control of Hazardous Energy	$29.95		
OSHA Control of Hazardous Energy Library Edition	$79.95		
OSHA Control of Hazardous Energy Manual and CD	$39.95		
OSHA Eye Safety	$49.95		
OSHA Eye Safety Library Edition	$99.95		
OSHA Eye Safety Manual and CD	$59.95		
OSHA Fire Safety	$49.95		
OSHA Fire Safety Library Edition	$99.95		
OSHA Fire Safety Manual and CD	$59.95		
OSHA Hazard Communications	$29.95		
OSHA Hazard Communications Library Edition	$79.95		
OSHA Hazard Communications Manual and CD	$39.95		
OSHA Management Certificate Program	$299.95		

Title Name	Price	Quantity	Total
OSHA Management Certificate Program Manual and CD	$319.95		
OSHA Management Program Library Edition	$399.95		
OSHA Medical Radiation Safety	$49.95		
OSHA Medical Radiation Safety Library Edition	$99.95		
OSHA Medical Radiation Safety Manual and CD	$59.95		
OSHA Medical Recordkeeping	$29.95		
OSHA Medical Recordkeeping Library Edition	$79.95		
OSHA Medical Recordkeeping Manual and CD	$39.95		
OSHA Occupational Radiation Safety	$49.95		
OSHA Occupational Radiation Safety Library Edition	$99.95		
OSHA Occupational Radiation Safety Manual and CD	$59.95		
OSHA Penalty Policies	$29.95		
OSHA Penalty Policies Library Edition	$79.95		
OSHA Penalty Policies Manual and CD	$39.95		
OSHA Repetitive Strain Injury	$49.95		
OSHA Repetitive Strain Injury Library Edition	$99.95		
OSHA Repetitive Strain Injury Manual and CD	$59.95		
OSHA Safe Lifting	$49.95		
OSHA Safe Lifting Library Edition	$99.95		
OSHA Safe Lifting Manual and CD	$59.95		
OSHA Workplace Violence	$49.95		
OSHA Workplace Violence Library Edition	$99.95		
OSHA Workplace Violence Manual and CD	$59.95		
Part 11 and Computer Validation	$299.95		
Part 11 and Computer Validation Library Edition	$449.95		
Part 11 and Computer Validation Manual and CD	$349.95		
Pharmaceutical Computer Validation Introduction	$99.95		
Pharmaceutical Computer Validation Introduction Library Edition	$199.95		
Pharmaceutical Computer Validation Introduction Manual and CD	$139.95		
Pharmaceutical Quality Control Lab	$149.95		
Pharmaceutical Quality Control Lab Library Edition	$249.95		
Pharmaceutical Quality Control Lab Manual and CD	$179.95		
Provider Patient Relationships	$49.95		
Provider Patient Relationships Library Edition	$99.95		
Provider Patient Relationships Manual and CD	$59.95		
Refraction 1 Introduction	$49.95		
Refraction 1 Introduction Library Edition	$99.95		
Refraction 1 Introduction Manual and CD	$59.95		
Reorganizing for Customer Care in Healthcare	$49.95		
Reorganizing for Customer Care in Healthcare Library Edition	$99.95		
Reorganizing for Customer Care in Healthcare Manual and CD	$59.95		
Sales Body Language	$49.95		
Sales Body Language Library Edition	$99.95		
Sales Body Language Manual and CD	$59.95		
Sales Humor Delivery Skills 1	$74.95		
Sales Humor Delivery Skills 1 Library Edition	$124.95		

Title Name	Price	Quantity	Total
Sales Humor Delivery Skills 1 Manual and CD	$84.95		
Sales Humor Writing Skills 1	$74.95		
Sales Humor Writing Skills 1 Library Edition	$124.95		
Sales Humor Writing Skills 1 Manual and CD	$84.95		
Secrets of a Leadership Coach	$199.95		
Secrets of a Leadership Coach 1 Executive Coaching Techniques	$49.95		
Secrets of a Leadership Coach 1 Executive Coaching Techniques Library Edition	$99.95		
Secrets of a Leadership Coach 1 Executive Coaching Techniques Manual and CD	$59.95		
Secrets of a Leadership Coach 2 Developing Ourselves as Leaders	$49.95		
Secrets of a Leadership Coach 2 Developing Ourselves as Leaders Library Edition	$99.95		
Secrets of a Leadership Coach 2 Developing Ourselves as Leaders Manual and CD	$59.95		
Secrets of a Leadership Coach 3 Developing Others	$49.95		
Secrets of a Leadership Coach 3 Developing Others Library Edition	$99.95		
Secrets of a Leadership Coach 3 Developing Others Manual and CD	$59.95		
Secrets of a Leadership Coach 4 Developing a Team	$49.95		
Secrets of a Leadership Coach 4 Developing a Team Library Edition	$99.95		
Secrets of a Leadership Coach 4 Developing a Team Manual and CD	$59.95		
Secrets of a Leadership Coach 5 Practice and Assessments	$49.95		
Secrets of a Leadership Coach 5 Practice and Assessments Library Edition	$99.95		
Secrets of a Leadership Coach 5 Practice and Assessments Manual and CD	$59.95		
Secrets of a Leadership Coach Library Edition	$299.95		
Secrets of a Leadership Coach Manual and CD	$219.95		
Surviving OSHA Inspections	$29.95		
Surviving OSHA Inspections Library Edition	$79.95		
Surviving OSHA Inspections Manual and CD	$39.95		
Writing Clearly	$49.95		
Writing Clearly Library Edition	$99.95		
Writing Clearly Manual and CD	$59.95		
Order Total			
California Sales Tax of 8.25%			
Shipping and Handling: 5% for the US, 10% outside the US. Add to Order Total.			
Grand Total (Order Total plus tax for California residents plus shipping)			

Credit Card: (Prices subject to change without notice. For Windows 95, 98, Me, 2000, XP only.)

Visa____ Mastercard____ American Express____ (Prices may change without notice.)

Expiration Date_____/_____ Card number _____

Name on Card_____Signature:_____

Address _____

City _____ State_____ Postal Code _____

Country _____ Phone _____

Send form with check or credit card information to OpAmp Technical Books, Los Angeles, CA 90038, USA. Fax: 323-927-1570. Questions: Call 323-937-4242. E-mail: lyn@ubc.com. You may also buy on the website link from http://www.uohc.com/CDROMs.htm. Note that all courses are licensed for one user on one computer at a time except for library editions, which allow two uses. Library editions are expected to be ready in January 2004.